The 1772 Philadelphia Furniture Price Book

AN INTRODUCTION AND GUIDE

Alexandra Alevizatos Kirtley

Philadelphia Museum of Art
in association with
Antique Collectors' Club Ltd

This publication was supported by an endowment for the Center for American Art at the Philadelphia Museum of Art.

The facsimile is a reproduction of *Prices of Cabinet and Chair Work*, 1772. Philadelphia Museum of Art. Partial and promised gift of Thomas S. Howland, Jr., and Dolores B. Howland in memory of Earl and Margaret McAllister. 2004-51-1

Produced by the Department of Publishing, Philadelphia Museum of Art
2525 Pennsylvania Avenue, Philadelphia, PA 19130, USA, www.philamuseum.org

Co-published by Antique Collectors' Club Ltd, www.antiquecc.com

Library of Congress Cataloging-in-Publication Data

The 1772 Philadelphia furniture price book : a facsimile / with an
introduction and guide by Alexandra Alevizatos Kirtley.
    p. cm. — (Primary sources in American art ; no. 2)
  Includes index.
  ISBN 0-87633-188-6 (pbk.)
  1. Furniture—Pennsylvania—Philadelphia—History—18th century—Catalogs.
I. Kirtley, Alexandra Alevizatos. II. Series.
  NK2438.P5A16 2005   749'.09748'11075—dc22   2005001478

Contents

Foreword

The number of highly skilled furniture craftsmen working in Philadelphia on the eve of the American Revolution created a confluence of artistic energy, the results of which can be seen today in the towering monuments of double-case pieces, the sinuous legs of dainty card and tea tables, and the welcoming seats of capacious armchairs, to cite just a few furniture forms. Philadelphia-made furniture from the third quarter of the eighteenth century tells a complex story of evolving tastes, styles, and techniques as well as economic opportunities in the city that was the center of the lively political discourse out of which a new republic was born.

Trained mostly in European urban centers, where strict guild systems governed craft apprenticeships, Philadelphia's furniture craftsmen were the first known to have published a guide that dictated retail prices for furniture and wages paid to journeymen. Known for a century through two incomplete manuscript copies, the printed version of the 1772 Philadelphia *Prices of Cabinet and Chair Work* came to light in the summer of 2003 when longtime Pennsylvania residents Tom and Dee

Howland discovered the small and wonderfully preserved copy in a box of books they had inherited in the 1960s. They consulted with a friend who led them to Lita Solis-Cohen, a knowledgeable and well-known author of articles on antiques, who has long been involved with the Philadelphia Museum of Art. Guided by Mrs. Solis-Cohen and furniture scholar Alan Miller to understand that the book would find its ideal home in the context of the Museum's extraordinary collection of American furniture, the Howlands decided to donate the book to the Museum. This remarkable treasure is now reprinted in facsimile as the second in a new series of small publications, Primary Sources in American Art, supported by the Center for American Art at the Museum. In her introductory essay, Assistant Curator of American Decorative Arts Alexandra Alevizatos Kirtley describes the aspects of eighteenth-century Philadelphia that inspired the creation of the price book, and her guide assists the reader in understanding the furniture options for which prices are given.

With the appearance of this illuminating little book, it is a pleasure to salute the donors, Mr. and Mrs. Howland; the acute eye and good friendship of Lita Solis-Cohen; and the generosity of Robert L. McNeil, Jr., whose keen interest in scholarship pertaining to the arts in Philadelphia has led to many distinguished publications over the decades and to the recent creation of the Center for American Art at this Museum.

ANNE D'HARNONCOURT
*The George D. Widener Director
and Chief Executive Officer
Philadelphia Museum of Art*

KATHLEEN A. FOSTER
*The Robert L. McNeil, Jr.,
Curator of American Art
and Director, Center for American Art*

The 1772 Price Book:
The Art and Economy of Furniture Making in Pre-Revolutionary Philadelphia

ALEXANDRA ALEVIZATOS KIRTLEY

Philadelphia in 1772—then the second-largest city in the British empire, after London—was a vibrant cultural center that was home to a large and sophisticated community of furniture craftsmen. These master craftsmen, some of whom were recent immigrants trained in the best shops in London, produced furniture that rivaled the finest imports, but they operated in an unregulated and sometimes chaotic marketplace with no guidelines for setting retail prices or paying the journeymen they hired to produce many of the components.[1] It was for this reason that a group of Philadelphia craftsmen that year published *Prices of Cabinet and Chair Work*, a thirty-six-page book listing the furniture they made along with suggested retail prices and the wages master furniture makers should pay journeymen for particular items.

Essentially an example of price fixing, the book established standard costs for furniture, through which the master furniture craftsmen sought to gain respect and power within the politically charged entrepreneurial economic climate of pre-Revolutionary Philadelphia. Set prices and wages also minimized competition, both among master craftsmen and between the masters and the journeymen.[2] The price book codified what had often been a verbal contract between the journeymen, who were expected to make a quality piece of furniture or its components, and the master craftsmen, who marketed and sold the finished product, paid the shop overhead and journeymen's wages, and frequently extended credit to the purchaser. Although the price guide limited the ability of the journeymen to sell their skills to the highest bidder, it also protected them against unscrupulous master craftsmen.[3]

While some standardization of prices within the craft had occurred in both Europe and America prior to 1772, the Philadelphia publication is the first furniture price book known to have been printed. The single surviving copy, now in the collection of the Philadelphia Museum of Art, contains fifty-six headings for furniture forms, including desks, bookcases, high chests, chairs, sofas, beds, clothes presses, and numerous tables for specialized uses. Listed below each heading are choices for variations in the design and styling, with three columns to the right giving the price to be charged for each option in mahogany or walnut as the primary wood and the amount that should be paid to the journeymen who produced the components, which were known as "piecework."[4]

Colonial American journeymen and master furniture makers were aware of the power European guild systems permitted their members in negotiating set retail prices and journeymen's wages. The first such agreement in America was established in Providence, Rhode Island, in a one-page manuscript entitled "Particular Price of Joinery Work," which listed thirty-five types of furniture and their retail prices. This 1756 document (with an addendum for inflated 1757 costs) was agreed upon by six furniture craftsmen who, at the bottom of the page, accepted wages for "Journeymen's work for making." This informal list stands in stark contrast to the sophistication of the price book printed in Philadelphia in 1772.[5]

The 1772 publication proved so successful in its organization and structuring of prices and wages that it endured over the next twenty years and provided a model for furniture price books published in London in 1788; Hartford, Connecticut, in 1792; and New York in 1796.[6] When Philadelphia's furniture makers decided in the early 1790s that the 1772 book had become obsolete, disputes erupted over the form a new version should take. Disagreements played out in lively exchanges in Philadelphia newspapers between the societies of the cabinet- and chair-makers and those of the journeymen.[7] The cabinet- and chair-makers even published unofficial "renegade" price books in which journeymen's wages were considerably lower, and they agreed unilaterally not to hire journeymen who were members of a society. Finally, in 1796, the parties agreed to use the prices for journeymen's wages set forth in a London publication of 1793, which was styled after the Philadelphia book of 1772. The compromise, which resulted in *The Cabinet-Makers' Philadelphia and London Book of Prices*, published by the Federal Society of Philadelphia Cabinet and Chair-makers in 1796, was perceived as a victory for the journeymen workers whose piecework proved crucial to the ability of the master craftsmen to make and sell finished wares.

✳ ✳ ✳ ✳ ✳

Until the printed copy now at the Museum was discovered in the summer of 2003, this publication was known only through two manuscript copies, one at the Historical Society of Pennsylvania in Philadelphia and one at the library of the Tyler Arboretum in Lima, Pennsylvania.[8] The Historical Society's manuscript was transcribed by Benjamin Lehman, a lumberyard owner, who signed his name and wrote only the date "1786" underneath the title "Prices of Cabinet and Chair Work" on the first page. The importance of the so-called Lehman price listing for furniture was recognized as early as 1904, when it first resurfaced. This manuscript is vital to our understanding of the printed version because it is the only copy that identifies the three columns as prices for mahogany, walnut, and journeymen's labor.[9] The copy discovered in the library of the Tyler Arboretum in the late 1970s contains not only the title "Prices of Cabinet and Chair Work" but also the rest of the information on the printed version's title page, which is missing from the Lehman manuscript: "Philadelphia / Printed by James Hum[phries, Junior,] at the loer Corner of Black hors Aley MDCCLXXII." By comparing the Lehman and Tyler versions it became apparent that both were transcribed from the same original, which was a 1772 printed book. Unlike the manuscript copies, which end with beds (page 28), the newly discovered printed original book of prices is complete, revealing the full range of furniture made by Philadelphia's cabinet- and chair-makers at the time.

When Tom and Dee Howland discovered this tiny but rich treasure in a box of books inherited from a family friend, they were entranced but did not fully comprehend its incredible significance. Curious and wise, the Howlands sought out a prominent journalist of American decorative arts, Lita Solis-Cohen. She in turn consulted a furniture scholar, Alan Miller, who quickly informed them all of the book's astonishing importance to the field. All of the parties involved recognized its value was highest as a tool of learning, and the owners made the generous decision to give it to the Philadelphia Museum of Art.[10]

This seemingly simple book of lists provides an extraordinary view into the world of furniture making in Philadelphia in the latter part of the eighteenth century. By quantifying what was valued in design and style based on the extra amount the patron was willing to pay for embellishments, the 1772 Philadelphia price book unveils the trade secrets—or "art and mystery," to use the language of contemporary apprenticeship agreements—of Philadelphia furniture making. Indicators of style in furniture are based on broadly accepted art historical definitions of, for example, baroque and rococo. By giving the actual cost of imbuing furniture with particular stylistic elements, the book of prices enables curators, collectors, and dealers—

indeed, all students of American furniture—to understand the relevance of Philadelphia furniture making and style in a broader context.

Unlike books of cabinet and chair prices printed in the 1780s and 1790s, where the purpose of the document, the intended audience, and the names of those responsible for its production are clearly stated on the title page, the 1772 Philadelphia version opens with thrilling immediacy but little explanation. By its very nature, this small volume was intended for use by a limited audience. Access to the price books printed in the 1790s was limited to paying members of the craftsmen's societies, a practice that likely originated with earlier manuscript price lists and certainly applied to the 1772 printed version. Fines were imposed if a master or journeyman disclosed to outsiders specific price information, or perhaps even the existence of the document itself. Journeymen who worked for non-member masters and masters who hired non-member journeymen were also fined. Through control of the market over time, the community of craftsmen hoped to motivate non-member masters and journeymen to join their respective organizations, work within the stated regulations, and fight for common goals. The need for confidentiality contributed to the rarity of this volume, and its clandestine nature also may account for the absence of information about the exact motives for and circumstances of its publication.

This quarto-size (3¾ x 6¼ inches) printed book was designed to fit into a waistcoat pocket. Marbleized papers cover the laminated papers that comprise the board covers on the front and back. The text is printed on five folded folios of laid (rag) paper that are sewn from front to back across the folios (rather than through the folios, which was the usual practice), about one-quarter inch in from the spine edge. The printer, James Humphreys, Jr., was an ardent loyalist who is known to have been in New York, New England, and Nova Scotia from 1778 to 1797. While in Philadelphia, Humphreys also published "Rules and Constitutions of the Society of the Sons of St. George" (1772) and a public broadside of porterage and carriage rates (1774) that, like the furniture book, sought to establish prices within a particular trade.

The name "Joseph Delavau," written in ink on the back pastedown, suggests the possible original owner of the Museum's copy of this secret text. This is likely the same cabinetmaker that furniture historian William MacPherson Hornor, Jr., referred to as Joseph Delaveau in his *Blue Book of Philadelphia Furniture*[11] and whose name shows up as "Delahoe" and "Delaveau" in census records. Below the name he has written "sehelf," perhaps a misspelling of "self" and Delavau's emphatic claim of the book as his. Above the name three sums are written: £6 15*s.* 10*d.*, £3 15*s.*, and £2 10*s.*[12] The name "Robert F. Reynolds" is written horizontally at least four times on the back pastedown. Delavau's daughter Mary married a Robert Reynolds, whose son Robert may have added these later marks. Written in ink on the front pastedown is "For D^r [Debtor] Cadwaleter / fire screen frame 1=3 wide / Long 1 6 / with a draw / the Screen it self 2 foot long."[13] This inscription suggests that the original owner of the book was hired to make one of the famous lavishly carved fire screens for the townhouse of John and Elizabeth Cadwalader on Second Street in Philadelphia. Six of these distinctive fire screens survive (see fig. 12), but only the one owned by the Metropolitan Museum of Art has a frame that measures 2 feet high, as given in Delavau's inscription.[14]

✳ ✳ ✳ ✳ ✳

The furniture descriptions in the book of prices, with measurements, structural elements, and ornamental details delineated, afford a detailed picture of the art and economy of furniture making in pre-Revolutionary Philadelphia. The price book functioned independently of contemporary design or pattern books, such as those produced by London cabinetmaker Thomas Chippendale (1718–1779), who promoted fashionable furniture designs when he published *The Gentleman and Cabinetmaker's Director of Household Furniture in the Most Fashionable Taste* in 1754, 1755, and 1763. Unlike the texts and engravings of ornate and highly stylized furniture in books such as Chippendale's, the furniture listed in the 1772 Philadelphia price book reveals the specific tastes of the local market.

Large case pieces—desks, bookcases, and chests of drawers—are listed first, followed by seating furniture, including chairs, sofas, and settees. These are followed in turn by the large variety of tables available—dining tables, card tables, Pembroke (breakfast) tables, corner tables, tea tables, folding stands, sideboards, tea kettle stands, dressing tables, writing tables, night tables, frames for marble slabs, pine kitchen tables, joint stools, fire screens, and dumbwaiters. The last thirteen pages list an assortment of forms—most of which were omitted from the manuscript copies—including bedsteads, clothes presses, cupboards, clock cases, bottle cases, tea boards, cornices, window blinds, picture frames, ironing boards, and coffins.

The price book reveals multiple layers of facts about the economic parameters within which artisans produced the furniture that is so revered today for its design, proportion, and carved decorations. Labor costs in Colonial America were higher than those in Europe since the colonies had a smaller population and fewer skilled artisans. In order to compete with imported furniture, however, master craftsmen could not afford to pass all of this increased cost to the consumer in the form of higher retail prices. And yet, despite the labor costs for each artisan—cabinet- or chair-maker, turner or carver—who collaborated to make furniture in eighteenth-century Philadelphia, the value of a particular piece was determined primarily by the quality of the wood used. A comparison between the retail prices and the wages paid to the journeymen underlines the investment a master craftsman made in the wood, a cost that was then transferred to the patron. For example, a back stool, or chair with an upholstered back and seat, cost £1 5s. in mahogany and £1 in walnut, but the journeyman was paid only 6 shillings for making it in either wood. Adding arms, which were entirely made of the primary wood, cost 15 shillings more in mahogany and 10 shillings more in walnut; for this time-consuming task, the journeyman received only an additional 4 shillings. In fact, the 15 shillings charged for a single set of mahogany arms were nearly equivalent to a journeyman's pay for the labor of making four complete cabriole-legged side chairs. Similarly, a mahogany frame for a marble slab cost £1 more than the same in walnut, the difference being almost double what the journeyman earned for making the entire table.

These craftsmen who worked with wood every day understood its functional and decorative properties and exploited them well. Master craftsman also knew what they could sell, and they deemed particular woods more appropriate for certain pieces of furniture. In the frames for marble slabs, for example, walnut was acceptable only for the plainest version; when decorative embellishments were added, such as commode (serpentine) rails or bases on the Marlborough feet and carved brackets between the legs and the rails, the frames are priced only in mahogany. China tables, china trays, tea kettle stands, card tables with round (or turret) corners, and commode dressing tables also are priced only in mahogany. Only mahogany and poplar are listed as primary woods for any part of a bedstead, though cedar was used for the carved cornices. The low chest of drawers on page 6 is the only piece of furniture listed with a price in walnut but not mahogany. The surprising inclusion of mahogany as a material for window blinds revises the earlier belief that this expensive wood was reserved either for large surfaces on which its "figure" (grain) achieved a lively visual effect or for wares in which its ease of carving was exploited. Pine was the primary wood for picture frames, utilitarian furniture such as kitchen tables, and furniture that may have been painted, such as chests and cupboards.

Journeymen commonly earned between 15 and 25 shillings for a day's work. The amount of time necessary to make the furniture described in the 1772 book of prices can therefore be calculated. A bureau table with a prospect door and square corners, for example, probably took a little over two days to make; add quarter columns to the order and the journeyman would have worked almost three days on the case piece.

❋ ❋ ❋ ❋ ❋

True artists in wood, Philadelphia's furniture craftsmen were nonetheless constrained by the need to sell furniture for profit. Thus, they paid close attention to evolving fashions, and the furniture they made reflected the aspirations of their cultured patronage. Wares made in Philadelphia in the third quarter of the eighteenth century competed well against imports from London, Continental Europe, and Asia.

The 1904 publication of portions of a manuscript copy of a list of prices for cabinet and chair work was the beginning of a quest to understand the economic forces that impelled these craftsmen to produce the furniture we treasure today. Hornor's reliance on that Lehman manuscript in his 1935 *Blue Book,* which remains the seminal work on Philadelphia furniture, shaped the minds of generations of furniture enthusiasts. The realization in the late 1970s that both the Lehman manuscript and the subsequently discovered Tyler manuscript were copied from a 1772 printed book of prices changed whole ways of thinking about the dating of furniture by style. The search for an original printed copy of Philadelphia's *Prices of Cabinet and Chair Work* ended in 2003 with the serendipitous discovery of the book reproduced here in facsimile, which has thirteen more pages accounting for fourteen additional items not included in the manuscript copies. This particular copy of the book was also signed by the cabinetmaker who owned it—Joseph Delavau—and bears his wonderful scribble about John Cadwalader's fire screen.

Today, the *Prices of Cabinet and Chair Work* is to be understood as a guide from which master cabinet- and chair-makers in Philadelphia in 1772 derived standards of finished work and paid their journeymen, and according to which journeymen demanded a standard of remuneration. The lucid descriptions allow anyone interested in the history of furniture to understand how the craftsmen broke down the components of the forms they made, to see what particular stylistic attributes cost in comparison with others, and to adopt the contemporary descriptive terminology used by these highly skilled artisans.

Notes

1. *Master craftsmen* were those who had successfully completed an apprenticeship and had opened their own shop. *Journeymen* had either completed an apprenticeship and not been able to open their own shop (perhaps because of lack of capital) or had learned the craft without having undergone an apprenticeship.
2. See Charles F. Montgomery, *American Furniture: The Federal Period in the Henry Francis du Pont Winterthur Museum* (New York: Viking, 1966), pp. 19–26. In Philadelphia in the second half of the eighteenth century, journeymen had begun to gain political power and were demanding better wages and conditions. See Gary B. Nash, "Artisans and Politics in Eighteenth-Century Philadelphia," in *The Craftsman in Early America,* ed. Ian M. G. Quimby (New York: W. W. Norton, 1984), pp. 62–88.

3. Philadelphia carpenters are known to have formed an association in 1732, and the publication of the 1772 price book represents solidarity among at least the master cabinet- and chair-makers. It is possible that Philadelphia journeymen were similarly united and that the wages listed in the 1772 book reflect their verbal agreements with the master craftsmen for various components. See Christopher Gilbert, "London and Provincial Books of Prices: Commentary and Bibliography," *Furniture History* 18 (1982), p. 1.

4. Secondary woods used in Philadelphia furniture in 1772 included yellow poplar, white and yellow pine, white and red cedar, ash, and oak. Brass hardware (usually imported) is not included in the prices.

5. Furniture craftsmen who emigrated from London may have based Philadelphia's printed version on manuscript books of prices that almost certainly existed in London before 1772.

6. See Montgomery, *American Furniture*, p. 19; Gilbert, "London and Provincial Books of Prices," pp. 11–16.

7. In general, cabinetmakers made casework and tables, while chair-makers made seating furniture. Certain components of all furniture (e.g., the turned elements of a chair or table) may have been provided to cabinet- and chair-makers by specialists. Wood turners sold piecework to some furniture makers, but masters and journeymen also had the tools and abilities to make certain turned parts. In later decades, Philadelphia journeymen sometimes signed and dated piecework. The author is currently researching this practice, which is not known in the 1770s.

8. See Martin Weil, "A Cabinetmaker's Price Book," *Winterthur Portfolio* 13 (1979), pp. 175–92.

9. See "The Furniture of Our Ancestors," *Pennsylvania Magazine of History and Biography* 28, nos. 1 and 2 (1904), pp. 78–83, 199–200. See also Harrold E. Gillingham, "Benjamin Lehman: A Germantown Cabinetmaker," *Pennsylvania Magazine of History and Biography* 54, no. 4 (1930), pp. 288–306; William MacPherson Hornor, Jr., "Fancy versus Facts," *Antiquarian* 15, no. 5 (November 1930), pp. 76, 108, 112. Hornor also used the Lehman manuscript as his guide in organizing the text and plates in his *Blue Book of Philadelphia Furniture: William Penn to George Washington (1682–1807)* (Philadelphia: published by the author, 1935).

10. See Lita Solis-Cohen, "Rosetta Stone for Philadelphia Furniture," *Maine Antique Digest*, March 2004, pp. 26D–27D. Alan Miller will publish an interpretive guide to the furniture described in the 1772 book of prices in *American Furniture*, an annual journal published by the Chipstone Foundation.

11. Hornor, *Blue Book of Philadelphia Furniture*, pp. 102, 322.

12. The currency abbreviations used herein are £ for British pounds, *s.* for shillings, and *d.* for pence.

13. The last two lines of the inscription are obscured by dark black ink added long after the words were written. Below the Cadwalader inscription and partially obscured by a later ink is "Mr. H. H. Brown ———ght chair to be done on Wednesday next." Below that is a silhouette of a man's head and, to the right, "1772" in script.

14. A bill dated October 13, 1770, records that among the furniture ordered to furnish the Cad-

waladers' townhouse, Thomas Affleck charged for "4 Mahogany fire screens @ 2..10" each, for a total of £10. According to the 1772 *Book of Prices*, the £2 10s. Affleck charged the Cadwaladers in 1770 was only the standard retail price for a less ornate fire screen; the fluted area above the turned and carved vase on the pole of the Cadwalader screens would have cost 5 shillings extra; the carving would have been done by a specialist and charged separately. A close analysis of the six surviving Cadwalader screens identified two different manufacturers for the four ordered in 1770 and another unrecorded order of at least two more screens. A seventh fire screen, though related to the Cadwalader screens in design, is likely not part of the group. See Mark J. Anderson, Gregory J. Landrey, and Philip D. Zimmerman, *Cadwalader Study* (Winterthur, Del.: The Henry Francis du Pont Winterthur Museum, 1995), pp. 24–30, tables 3–5, and figs. 11–20. The extra carving and cost of the hairy paw feet on the Cadwalader screens was charged separately. See Nicholas B. Wainwright, *Colonial Grandeur in Philadelphia* (Philadelphia: Historical Society of Pennsylvania, 1964), p. 44.

CASE FURNITURE

Desks (*p. 2*). Each entry in the price book for a "desk" assumes the standard form of a hinged and slanted fall front that, when opened, serves as a writing surface; a fitted interior; and a case of drawers underneath. The first, and also most expensive (£14), is the "winged" desk. This perplexing description has given rise to misunderstanding—Hornor conceived of it as having flanking bookcases.[1] The term "winged" actually describes the interior of the desk, in which an end stack of drawers extends beyond the plane of the central prospect.[2] A desk interior with "scalloped" (serpentine) drawers (fig. 1) surmounted by shell drawers, but with no winged sides, was available for £13 10s. Quarter columns on the front corners of the case of drawers, an element common but not necessarily distinctive to Philadelphia casework, could also be chosen as an option. Narrow vertical "column drawers" on either side of the desk interior prospect (or center door) were used to store documents. A "sliding prospect," or removable center interior section, provided a secret place to store valuables. Desks could have either swelled-bracket feet with a baroque ogee, or S-curve, shape (see fig. 1), or "straight" brackets that were more in keeping with the rising preference for neoclassical styles.

Bookcases (*pp. 2–3*). The expense of bookcases lay in the elaborate designs for the "heads," or tops, and doors. The available ornamentation for the heads included straight molding, sawn openwork interlaced frets applied to flat friezes, soaring pitch pediments with dentils (teeth-like decoration) or balls underneath the moldings, and arched or scrolled pediments, all of which mimic architectural designs of Greek and Roman temples. The doors on bookcases could be, in order of cost, plain, paneled or sashed, arch-topped, or scalloped. The most expensive choices for doors were the elaborate Chinese-inspired mullioned doors (see fig. 1).

High Chests of Drawers (pp. 3–5). The high chest of drawers was a two-case form comprised of a chest of drawers on a table frame with drawers. This long entry (nearly three pages) includes not only the two-part high chest (fig. 2) but also the accompanying dressing table (fig. 3); a standard chest of drawers, essentially comprised of the upper case of drawers with feet; and a chest-on-chest, which consisted of two chests of drawers on top of one another, the lower one with feet. Quarter columns on the front

corners of both the table and the chest were among the extra-cost options, as were swelled-bracket (ogee, or S-curve) feet and additional drawers. Fluting the quarter columns, or making vertical concave undulations around the column's surface, would also have been an extra cost. A drawer fitted with desk partitions and compartments and with a hinged drop-down front could be added to any chest for the considerable sum of £3. Some carved elements, such as the center shield of the pediment on the upper cases of high chests and chests-on-chests, were made in the cabinet shop by specialists whose fees are specified in the price book, while other carving was charged separately.

Low Chest of Drawers (p. 6). Priced only in walnut, the low chest of drawers was a vernacular storage chest with three or four long drawers surmounted by five small drawers. An 18-inch-high frame to support the chest cost 10 shillings extra.

Fig. 1. Desk and Bookcase, made in Philadelphia, c. 1762. Mahogany, white cedar, yellow poplar, yellow pine, glass. The desk sits on swelled-bracket feet and its interior has a central prospect (door open), column drawers, and scalloped drawers that are not winged. The bookcase has a pitch pediment head, dentils, fret and shield, and Chinese glazed doors.

Fig. 2. High Chest of Drawers, Thomas Tufft (American, d. 1793), made in Philadelphia, 1773–85. Mahogany, yellow poplar, yellow pine, white cedar. The scroll pediment head of this high chest has extra carved work. Both the high chest and dressing table (fig. 3) have quarter columns.

Fig. 3. Dressing Table, Thomas Tufft, made
in Philadelphia, 1773–85. Mahogany,
yellow poplar, yellow pine, white cedar.

No embellishments such as swelled-bracket feet, quarter columns on the corners, or a drawer in the frame are priced out for this form.

SEATING FURNITURE

Chairs with Crooked Legs (pp. 6–7). Side chairs, armchairs, and corner chairs were available with crooked, or cabriole, legs; their seats could be upholstered with leather, damask (probably worsted wool or a wool blend), or hair. The "knees," or tops of the legs, could be carved with leaves or shells, as could the front rail of the seat, all for additional cost. The option of "relieving the banisters" would be better understood today as a strapped, or interlaced, splat (fig. 4). Such designs were sawn and carved. Customers might also choose to have the stiles (outer posts of the chair back) fluted or ogee-shaped. Rather than quoting a price for carving the undecorated surfaces, the book instructs that "[f]or any extraordinary carved work" performed in the shop (possibly by a hired specialist carver), the master craftsman should "add in proportion," implying that patrons desired, and local carvers provided, a range in quantity and quality. Extra cost was required to make an armchair and also to add a frame inside the seat rails to transform the chair into a "close-stool" designed to hold a chamber pot.

Chairs with Marlborough Feet (pp. 7–8). The placement of chairs with Marlborough feet—that is, those with straight or sometimes tapered legs—after crooked-leg chairs may indicate the relative popularity of the former, which survive in larger numbers. In the 1772 price book, Marlborough-legged chairs with "bases" (2- to 3-inch moldings added to make spade feet) were an option only if the patron also chose sawn and carved brackets (nailed where the legs meet the rails) and, on armchairs, fluted or ogee-shaped stiles.[3] As on the crooked-leg

Fig. 4. Side Chair, made in Philadelphia, 1765–75. Mahogany, yellow pine. The banister, or splat, of this chair is relieved with an interlaced strapwork design that was first sawn and then carved.

chairs, an additional (but unspecified) expense was required for such extras as sawn or pierced splats ("relieving the banister"), damask or horsehair slip seats (bottoms), or seats fitted with a chamber-pot frame. A stylish option priced out on Marlborough but not crooked-leg chairs was to have the seat upholstery "stuffed over the rail," with brass nails, a feature that was customary on easy chairs but extraordinary on side chairs and armchairs.[4]

Corner Chairs (pp. 8–9). A corner chair designed to hold a close-stool received its own heading, most likely because it had high rails shaped to disguise the chamber pot. Straight legs on plain feet; straight legs on ball-and-claw feet (simply called "claw feet"); a pierced, or open, splat; and crooked legs were among the options. A "commode front," or rounded and serpentine rails, added 12 shillings to the retail cost in mahogany, 10 in walnut.

Easy Chairs (pp. 9–10). The easy chair frame described in the 1772 price book was relatively inexpensive and could be designed with the usual choices: crooked or Marlborough legs, plain or carved knees, plain or claw feet, with or without casters (fig. 5). The *chair frame* "for stuffing over back and seat, with Marlborough feet," describes what is known as a back stool (fig. 6); a back stool with arms was also known as an elbow, or French, chair. Back stools and easy chair frames as described cost relatively little because the expense of these luxurious items was in their upholstery and wool or silk show covers, which were products of a wholly separate craft. Folding cabin chairs with stuffed and upholstered seats were used as outdoor furniture and on private schooners. For additional cost, brackets, bases (spade feet) on straight Marlborough legs, and carved moldings could be added to any of the above.

Fig. 5. Easy Chair, made in Philadelphia, 1755–65.
Mahogany, oak, yellow pine, yellow poplar.

Fig. 6. Back Stool, made in Philadelphia, 1760–70.
Mahogany, oak, yellow pine. Unlike many surviving
examples, this chair has the original decorative
corner brackets.

Sofas (pp. 10–11). Essentially longer versions of easy chairs, sofas had frames with shaped crests and scrolled ends (arms) of the same height, with the seat, ends, and back all to be upholstered. They could feature either crooked or Marlborough legs and were available with the same options as easy chairs: plain or carved knees, plain or claw feet, and carved moldings on crooked-leg examples; bases (spade feet), brackets, frets, and carved moldings on Marlborough-leg examples. Both types could be had with casters for an extra 10 shillings. As with easy chairs, the exorbitant expense of sofas lay in the cost of upholstering them, which is not addressed in the price book.

Settees (p. 11). Settees had backs consisting of several chair splats sharing a single crest rail and seats measuring the length of two to three chairs. The legs could be crooked or Marlborough and the back splats could be as plain or as ornate as desired. The addition of a carved molding earned the journeyman 20 shillings but interestingly did not increase the cost of the settee.

Couches (p. 12). Often called a "daybed," the couch described in the 1772 book of prices had a splat back at one end and a seat that was long enough to accommodate a person lying down. Its long surface was covered with a generously stuffed and upholstered cushion appropriately called a mattress, since the couch was used as a day lounger or optional bed for houseguests. It was available with a solid or carved open-banister splat; fluted or ogee-shaped stiles; and plain or carved crooked legs ending in plain, claw, or Marlborough feet, with or without bases and brackets. Mahogany frames for the seat surface were available with carved moldings underneath for an extra 20 shillings, of which the journeyman received only 2 shillings.

Dining Tables (pp. 12–13). Dining tables were distinguished by having two drop leaves. They were priced according to the size of the "bed," or framed box underneath the fixed surface, which determined the size of the leaves and thus of the table itself. The bed had both fixed rails and hinged rails that swung out to support the leaves. Dining tables were available either with crooked legs and plain feet or with Marlborough legs and bases; each claw foot added *2s. 6d.* For Marlborough legs with no bases, the book instructs the craftsman to "deduct *5s.* and *3s.* in journeyman's wages."

Card Tables (pp. 13–14). Similar to dining tables, card tables had a bed or box from which at least one of the legs swung out to support a hinged leaf that folded over the fixed top. Unlike the larger and usually oblong dining tables, however, the card tables were smaller and more likely to be square when opened. Less expensive card tables had plain legs, knees, and feet and no textile sunk into the open playing surface. More ornate tables might have carved knees and claw feet or bases and brackets. A carved or shaped molding cost extra but would have added significantly to the overall visual effect of the table, especially when it was closed and the horizontal lines of the table were doubly strong. Adding round (or ovolo) corners created a turret-like effect (fig. 7) but also added greatly to the cost of the table; even with plain knees and feet, the extra wood and labor needed to create round corners made such card tables cost £1 more than the most ornate straight-railed card table.

Pembroke (Breakfast) Tables (pp. 14–15). The table that still bears the name Pembroke—after the Countess of Pembroke, England, who apparently first ordered one like it—is distinguished by having

Fig. 7. Card Table, made in Philadelphia, 1755–65. Mahogany, yellow poplar, yellow pine, oak, white cedar. Candlesticks were placed in the corners to illuminate the playing surface.

two hinged flaps underneath the bed that support small leaves on either side. Also referred to as breakfast tables, Pembroke tables usually measured about 3½ feet wide by 3 feet long when opened. For additional cost, they could be ordered with a drawer at one or at both ends; with crooked legs and plain or claw feet; or with Marlborough legs that had bases and brackets. The tables could also have stretchers between the legs to provide extra support; these could be plain with molded edges or have decorative sawn or pierced openings. The leaves could be scalloped, with serpentine ends shaped like mouse ears and resembling the round corners on the card table.

Corner Tables (p. 15). Another variant on the hinged-top table was the corner table, in which a three-sided "box" was oriented diagonally to the top and the leaf was hinged across the long side. The table was triangular when folded up and could be stored in the corner of a room. As with the other tables, the patron could choose the type of legs and feet.

Tea Tables (pp. 15–16). As defined by the 1772 Philadelphia book of prices, a tea table had a round top attached by a block to a straight pedestal, or pillar, and supported by low, crooked legs (plain or leaf carved), which could end in either plain or claw feet (fig. 8). The top was hinged and tilted up from the pillar for easy storage. Both the top and pillar were turned; given the long history of this craft in Philadelphia, the journeyman's wage listed in the price book may have been for a wood-turner specially hired by the master craftsman. The top of the tea table could have a plain edge or a scalloped and carved one with flourishes; the latter option, when combined with a carved pillar, added almost £2 to the cost of the table. The carving of the scalloped edge may have been hired out to a specialist. No price is added for so-called birdcage boxes

Fig. 8. Tilt-top Tea Table, William Savery (American, 1721/22–1787), made in Philadelphia, 1750–70. Mahogany.

underneath, which permitted the top to rotate while it was horizontal.

Folding Stands (p. 16). A folding stand was a diminutive tilt-top table, with a top that measured either 18 or 22 inches in diameter. A small box was used in place of the large block that joined the round tilt-top to the pillar on the larger tables. Interestingly, to carve flutes into the pillar cost the same amount on the small stand as it did on the larger table (5 shillings retail, with *2s. 6d.* going to the journeyman).

Sideboard Tables (pp. 16–17). Used in dining rooms for displaying equipage and serving food, the sideboard table was just coming into fashion in 1772 as a long, low table, without the cellarette boxes that later became ubiquitous on sideboards. The design variations are limited in the 1772 book of prices. All sideboard tables listed had straight Marlborough legs, bases, and brackets; the only variation was the size, which ranged from 6 feet long by 2½ feet deep to 3 feet long by 2¼ feet deep. Carved moldings and frets were charged by the linear foot (fig. 9).

Tea Kettle Stands (p. 17). Small tea kettle stands were designed to hold elaborate hot water urns, especially those made of silver. The stands had one stationary surface enclosed by a fret-sawn gallery on a single turned pillar. The galleries were highly decorative and also prevented the hot water urn from sliding off the small top. No Philadelphia examples of this formal stand are known to survive. Also listed with the tea kettle stand is the utilitarian "bason" (washbasin) stand, which had either a round or square top above two drawers and was supported by three pillars.

Square Tea Tables (p. 18). Square tea tables were not nearly as common in Philadelphia as the round

Fig. 9. Sideboard Table, made in Philadelphia, 1765–75. Mahogany, yellow pine, white cedar. According to the 1772 prices, this sideboard would have cost £5.

Fig. 10. Tea Table, attributed to Benjamin Randolph (American, 1721–1791); made in Philadelphia, 1765–75. Mahogany, cherry, white cedar. Carved on three sides only, this extraordinary table was intended to be placed against a wall. It was made for Vincent Loockerman of Dover, Delaware.

tilt-top tables listed earlier, but they are still included in the 1772 price book. The term *square* did not necessarily refer to the equal measurement of the sides, but rather to the perpendicular corners, achieved through the use of a T-square. Square tea tables are listed only with cabriole legs; the rails, knees, and feet could be plain or carved. The Philadelphia Museum of Art owns an extraordinary example of this rare Philadelphia type (fig. 10).

Commode Dressing Tables (p. 18). No Philadelphia examples of the commode dressing table described in the price book, with serpentine top rails and drawers, are known to survive. It was designed with four long drawers that were not intended to extend the full height of the case; instead, the open area beneath the drawers and framed by the legs would have given the chest a lighter appearance. Although popular in Europe, this form was likely rarely made in Philadelphia due to its high price. For the £14 cost of the commode table without a dressing drawer, one could have had a high chest and dressing table. The uppermost dressing drawer, with partitions for jewelry, make-up, peruke (wig) and hair accouterments, and often a mirror supported by a ratcheted frame, could add up to £4 to the cost.

Writing Tables (p. 19). Like sideboards, writing tables were a form that was just evolving in 1772. These rather expensive items looked like tables with writing boxes on top. The price book describes them as having either a hinged top that could be raised on one side, or, for an additional 10 shillings, one that opened on both sides. A table with two tops that could be raised on either side was also available. The interior of the pull-out drawer could be suited to the patron's individual taste. That work was probably contracted out to a "cabinet smalls" specialist, who would charge separately for it.

Bureau Tables (p. 19). Bureau tables had one or two storage drawers and a small open bookshelf situated at the back edge of the top that was fitted with pigeonholes and possibly a prospect door in the center. Expensive and jewel-like in their design and decoration, these tables would be in high demand as the neoclassical style gained popularity in the 1780s.

China Tables (pp. 19–20). Perhaps the most self-consciously ostentatious of furniture, china tables were specifically designed to show off an owner's collection of porcelain in the most refined way. These tables, by definition, boasted straight Marlborough legs with brackets at the top, stretchers, and a fret-sawn gallery top and were available only in the more expensive mahogany. The stretchers and rails could be pierced, or fret-sawn, to add to the table's delicate elegance. Commode, or serpentine, rails added £2 10s. to the already dear price of £8.

No Philadelphia tables matching the 1772 price book description are known to survive.

Night Tables (p. 20). A plain, unadorned night table used to store a chamber pot was one of the more ubiquitous furniture items offered in the price book. Its cost of £4 in mahogany and £3 5s. in walnut is seemingly high for a plain, utilitarian form. Much of that cost, however, was in the secondary wood— likely an aromatic mahogany or cedar.

Frames for Marble Slabs (p. 20). Often made entirely of elaborately carved components, frames for marble slabs supported heavy, expensive, and, in many cases, imported pieces of stone, off of which punch and other refreshments were served in the homes of the elite (fig. 11). The price book lists a frame with plain Marlborough legs "about 4 feet long," suggesting that these items were often sized to suit a specific piece of marble. Familiar stylistic

Fig. 11. Marble-topped Pier Table, made in Philadelphia, 1765–75. Mahogany, mahogany veneer, white cedar, marble top (replaced). This frame features commode rails.

variations—bases and brackets for the Marlborough legs, plain or carved for the crooked legs, carved moldings, and commode rails—were available for additional cost. Only the plainest table frame was priced in walnut; all other variations were in mahogany.

Pine Kitchen Tables (p. 21). Most middle-class Philadelphia homes likely had pine kitchen tables. Two sizes are given in the price book: one 4 feet long, with either two drawers and two leaves or one drawer and one leaf; and one 3½ feet long, with two leaves, one leaf, or one drawer. A pine kitchen table without a drawer cost a mere 12 shillings, again illustrating how much walnut and mahogany accounted for the high cost of the more formal furniture.

Joint Stools (pp. 21–22). A joint stool with a 3-foot-long sliding top was another basic piece of furniture that served as a table and a seat, with an optional drawer below the top surface for storage. The legs were likely turned, with stretchers between them, and the top given a rounded molded edge. This inexpensive item is priced in the walnut column, although based on price comparisons and surviving examples it was likely made of pine.

Fire Screens (p. 22). Fire screens shielded one's face from the heat produced by the large blaze needed to warm an entire room (fig. 12). With a design similar to that of a tilt-top tea table, the fire screen consisted of a framed piece of needlework or other textile mounted on a turned pole that ended on low cabriole legs, priced here with plain or clawed feet, plain or leaf-carved knees, and a plain or fluted pillar. A small variation—the *horse fire screen*—had the piece of textile suspended between two upright supports. A fret-sawn stretcher (rather than a plain one) at the base between the two uprights added to the cost.

Fig. 12. Fire Screen, shop of Thomas Affleck (American, born Scotland, 1740–1795); made in Philadelphia, 1771. Mahogany. This is one of the six surviving fire screens that stood in the fabled Philadelphia townhouse of John and Elizabeth Lloyd Cadwalader.

Dumbwaiters (pp. 22–23). The type of dumbwaiter described in the price book also derived its design from the tilt-top table. Dumbwaiters had tiered table surfaces upon which food being served was placed. A single turned pillar ending in low cabriole legs held four round, turned tops, possibly of graduated size. Philadelphia-made examples as described here have not been identified, perhaps because the lack of secondary wood on the form makes it difficult to tell where surviving examples originated.

MISCELLANEOUS ITEMS

Clothes Presses (pp. 23–24). A "cloaths" press, intended for storing textiles, consisted of two cases: the upper case had two doors that opened to sliding shelves, also called ledge trays; the lower case had three long drawers. The aromatic red cedar used as the secondary wood distinguished the clothes press from other double-case pieces and signified its use for long-term storage, perhaps off season. When the secondary wood was not red cedar, the cost decreased by a staggering £2. Adding a pitch pediment with dentils, a sawn and applied fret around the cornice, and a carved shield cost £6 extra; adding only the pitch pediment was an additional 10 shillings.

Cupboards (pp. 24–26). Cupboards are given in three variations: corner cupboards, single cupboards, and pine cupboards. The *corner cupboard* resembled a bookcase and, with parallel embellishments, cost about the same. This 7-foot-high cupboard consisted of an upper and lower case and was angled at the rear to fit into the corner of a room. Shoe molding, or raised molding at the base of the cupboard that matched that of the room in which it was placed, made it appear to be part of the original architectural design. The lower case had paneled doors, while the upper case could have paneled or glazed (mullioned) doors and a wide variety of pediment decorations. The most elegant corner cupboard had a scrolled pediment ending in carved roses, dentil decoration, a sawn fret on the straight cornice, a center shield, and two blazes (shield finials) on the ends. Made all in mahogany and with scalloped paneled doors, such a corner cupboard would cost £16; that same cupboard with glazed sash doors in a Chinese-inspired mullion pattern cost £15 10s. Corner cupboards in particular were considered highly architectonic and thus were distinguished from the cases pieces described in the beginning of the book. A *single cupboard* (sometimes called a *low cupboard*) was 4 feet high and could have been hung on a wall. It was not priced to have elaborate pediments; in mahogany and with dentils and paneled doors, it cost at most £5 10s. *Pine cupboards* were available in single and double versions. The double pine cupboard stood 7 feet high (like the corner cupboard), with double doors and no embellishments. The single pine cupboard was 4 feet high and was probably hung on a wall or set on a table. A pine cupboard was likely intended to be painted.

Clock Cases (p. 26). To the high cost of acquiring a clock movement, eighteenth-century patrons could add the considerable expense of the clock case. A case with a flat head (what is today called a hood or bonnet) was the least expensive. Heads with scrolled pediments ending in carved rosettes, sawn frets, dentils, shields, and blazes as well as turned and fluted columns flanking the clock face added significantly to the cost, though the narrow width of a clock case kept the price of the carved flourishes lower than similar elements on wider case pieces. The types of clock case feet—ogee bracket, straight bracket, crooked, or architectural base molding—are not mentioned.

Bedsteads (pp. 26–28). The section on bedsteads opens, appropriately, with a person's first and smallest bed—the cradle, which could be had in mahogany or walnut; carving is not priced but could have been added by a specialist. Elaborations and excessive costs for cradles, as for all bedsteads, were in the textiles that dressed them. Most full-size adult bedsteads are priced only in mahogany, sometimes with the local and widely used yellow (or tulip) poplar for the head posts and headboard, which were stained to look like mahogany and would have been concealed behind drapes and trimmings supplied by an upholsterer. The least expensive were low-post bedsteads with mahogany claw feet, followed by high-post bedsteads in poplar stained to look like mahogany, and finally high-post bedsteads with poplar head posts and headboards and mahogany foot posts; each type had options for various carved features. Gothic pillars, available on both poplar and mahogany bedsteads, were turned and carved posts ending in Marlborough legs with bases that looked like the quatrefoil-bundled columns in a Gothic cathedral. A field bedstead was collapsible and had canopy rails for privacy. Poplar bedsteads were the least expensive option, especially those with corded mattress supports.

China Trays (pp. 28–29). An accompaniment to the fashionable eighteenth-century custom of tea drinking, china trays were made entirely of mahogany. The trays measured 18 by 24 inches and could be had with commode (serpentine) sides for an extra £1—a one-third increase in price. Costs are also listed for a less sophisticated tray to hold a pewter service and a small caddy-like tray to carry knives and forks.

Tea Boards (p. 29). Included under the heading "Tea Boards" are the costs of scalloping the tops of tilt-top tables (see *Tea Tables*, above); turning a plain top for a stand (see *Folding Stands*, above); and turning small hand trays and decanter stands, or coasters.

Cornices (pp. 29–30). Cornices for beds—open carved (i.e., pierced, like fine picture frames) and with pulleys into which an upholsterer would gather the cords used to raise and lower bed curtains— were made of cedar to provide aromatic remedy to stuffy bedrooms. Such cornices could be stained or covered entirely with a rich textile glued to the carved elements. Window cornices, which could be carved, shaped, or plain and had pulley systems, were made of pine, as were other, less ornate bed cornices.

Window Blinds (p. 30). Window (venetian) blinds were regularly advertised by cabinet- and chair-makers of the mid to late eighteenth century, but the use of mahogany and walnut in their construction was not realized until the discovery of this book.

Plain Bed Rails (p. 31). Plain bed rails were the alternative to carved and shaped bed canopy cor-nices. In pine, they could be had with or without pulleys for upholstered bed curtains. Plain rails were also used on windows to provide a surface for pul-leys that raised and lowered upholstered coverings.

Store Double Desks (p. 31). A store double desk, designed for use in a merchant's shop, was oriented for two people to sit face to face. It had four legs, a single row of two or three drawers, and pigeonholes dividing the writing surface. The patron could dictate whether the height accommodated a standing or sitting person. The store double desk was quoted only in walnut and pine, with the latter costing one-third as much as walnut. The single desk was available in pine only.

Screens (p. 32). Paneled screens made of half-inch-thick boards were placed around fireplaces to shield the intense heat; they were charged by the leaf, or vertical panel, which measured 6 feet 2 inches high

by 2 feet 2 inches wide, and multiple leaves would be
hinged. Such screens could be upholstered either in
textile or in tooled leather, or they could be painted.

Picture Frames (pp. 32–33). In contemporary
Philadelphia estate inventories, elaborately carved
and gilded picture frames were often valued higher
than the works they framed.[5] The book of prices,
however, lists costs only for plain frames, stained
black and without carved work, with the rates determined by linear feet. The cost is listed in the walnut
column, but practice, precedent, and surviving
frames indicate that these most likely would have
been made of pine. Works of art to be framed man-
dated different mounts and finishes, such as a
wooden backing board, a pasted paper backing
board, or glass, all of which are priced here. Maps,
popularly hung on the walls of passages, offices, and
libraries, were often framed with a molded stretcher
on the top and bottom edges, at a cost of *3s. 9d.*

Ironing Boards (p. 33). Ironing boards were offered
only in cedar, a wood whose natural aroma was also
exploited for linen drawers, night tables, and bed
cornices. Rates were set by size; trussels that supported the board added 5 shillings to the cost.

Chests (pp. 33–34). The chests listed near the end of
the book of prices denote low storage chests, popularly known as blanket chests, whose tops opened
with a hinge in the back. In pine, these chests were
often painted with initials and commemorative decoration associated with marriage dowries, but they
were also available in more expensive walnut, aromatic red cedar, and mahogany. The type of hardware used—snip bills and common lock—is denoted
here for the first time. Drawers beneath the case and
shaped bracket feet also added to the cost.

Bottle Cases (p. 34). Bottle cases with partitions in
which to store wine and liquor were available in

mahogany, walnut, and pine. All such cases had bracket feet, and little variation is given, suggesting that they did not have the ornamentation, such as lids and casters, found on later bottle cases.

Claw Feet (p. 35). The cost of laying out and cutting claw feet is priced out in a separate entry. Modern collectors value the style and quality of claw feet far beyond the effort that was actually put into their making in the eighteenth century. In the shop of a master cabinet- and chair-maker, cutting the claw feet was delegated to journeymen, whose proficiency set a standard in each of the urban centers. Claws for tables, chairs, tea tables, and chests (cases) of drawers earned the journeyman a mere 1*s.* 6*d.* each. Bedsteads required larger legs and more substantial feet and paid 2 shillings each. Small candle, kettle, and fire screen stands, with their shorter legs, did not necessitate large claw feet and paid 1*s.* 9*d.* each.

Coffins (pp. 35–36). Eighteenth-century cabinet-makers not only sold coffins but, along with upholsterers, also acted as funeral directors, preparing the body and arranging the viewing, funeral procession, and burial—although prices for these services are not included here. The prices for coffins are given in pine in the left column, with the wage paid to the journeyman in the middle column. Coffins in red cedar or mahogany are listed at the end of the entry, with the price being the same for both woods. Coffins could be as ornate or as plain as the deceased or the survivors could afford. Options included tin or silver lacquered handles; lace covers; and the deceased's initials or name added to the side, perhaps carved. Fully trimmed coffins would have been upholstered inside; adding haircloth over the muslin-covered under-upholstery was another extravagance. Options for the upholstery of the coffins are given, suggesting that the furniture craftsman could also provide this service. Children's coffins were charged according to size. While the cost of arranging a child's funeral historically was not charged to the grieving parents, the cost of a coffin was. Especially in the eighteenth century, the rate of infant mortality necessitated that practice.[6] Appropriately, the rates for coffins are the final entry listed in the 1772 book of prices.

Notes

1. Hornor, *Blue Book of Philadelphia Furniture*, pl. 256.
2. The realization of the meaning of "winged" in this context was derived with the assistance of Dennis A. Carr. This interior is known in earlier desks, but is not common in surviving examples contemporary with the price book.
3. Spade feet, or capped bases, were tapered slightly and were higher than they were wide.
4. More Marlborough-leg chairs are upholstered half over the rail, but this style is also known on crooked-leg chairs, such as the Cadwalader saddle-seat chair of 1770. See Jack L. Lindsey and Darrel Sewell, "The Cadwalader Family: Art and Style in Early Philadelphia," *Philadelphia Museum of Art Bulletin*, vol. 91, nos. 384–85 (Fall 1996), p. 19, fig. 18.
5. For examples, see ibid., pp. 21–22, figs. 22–24.
6. The author thanks Dr. Anita Schorsch and Gary Buss for providing her with this information.

Index to the Price Book

List of Illustrations

Philadelphia Museum of Art. Purchased with the Thomas Skelton Harrison Fund, the George W. B. Taylor Fund, and the Joseph E. Temple Fund, and with the partial gift of Brian Topping, 2000-58-1.

Fig. 7. Card Table, Philadelphia, 1755–65. Mahogany, yellow poplar, yellow pine, oak, white cedar; 29⅝ x 35 x 33½ inches (75.2 x 88.9 x 85.1 cm). Philadelphia Museum of Art. Purchased with the John D. McIlhenny Fund, 1967-69-1.

Fig. 8. Tilt-top Tea Table, William Savery (American, 1721/22–1787), Philadelphia, 1750–70. Mahogany, 29½ x 34⅟₁₆ x 34⅞ inches (75 x 86.5 x 88 cm). Philadelphia Museum of Art. Purchased with the Haas Community Fund and the J. Stogdell Stokes Fund, 1968-174-1.

Fig. 9. Sideboard Table, Philadelphia, 1765–75. Mahogany, yellow pine, white cedar; 33¾ x 73¼ x 28½ inches (85.7 x 186.1 x 72.4 cm). Philadelphia Museum of Art. Purchased with the Thomas Skelton Harrison Fund, 1949-87-1.

Fig. 10. Tea Table, attributed to Benjamin Randolph (American, 1721–1791); Philadelphia, 1765–75. Mahogany, cherry, white cedar; 29½ x 26 x 18 inches (74.9 x 66 x 45.7 cm). Philadelphia Museum of Art. Gift of H. Richard Dietrich, Jr., 1974-223-1.

Fig. 11. Marble-topped Pier Table, Philadelphia, 1765–75. Mahogany, mahogany veneer, white cedar, marble top (replaced); 33¼ x 48½ x 25¼ inches (84.5 x 123.2 x 64.1 cm). Philadelphia Museum of Art. Purchased with the Joseph E. Temple Fund, 1922-85-1.

Fig. 12. Fire Screen, shop of Thomas Affleck (American, born Scotland, 1740–1795); Philadelphia, 1771. Mahogany, 62¼ x 19 x 17½ inches (158.1 x 48.3 x 44.5 cm). Philadelphia Museum of Art. Gift of Mrs. Harry A. Batten in memory of her husband, 1967-266-1.

Edited by David Updike

Production by Richard Bonk

Designed by Greer Allen

Color photography of *Prices of Cabinet and Chair Work* by Gavin Ashworth

Black-and-white photography by Christie's, Inc. (fig. 2); Eric Mitchell (fig. 10); and Graydon Wood (figs. 1, 3–6, 8, 12)

Color separations by Streamline Press, North Branford, Connecticut

Printed and bound by CS Graphics, PTE, Ltd., Singapore

PRICES

OF

CABINET

AND

CHAIR WORK.

❈❈❈❈❈❈❈❈❈❈❈❈❈❈❈❈❈❈❈❈❈❈❈❈❈❈

PHILADELPHIA:

PRINTED BY JAMES HUMPHREYS, JUNIOR, IN FRONT-STREET, AT THE LOWER COR-
NER OF BLACK-HORSE ALLEY. M,DCC,LXXII.

1772

DESKS.

	£.	s.	d.	£.	s.	d.	£.	s.	d.
DESK, winged - - -	14	0	0	10	0	0	4	10	0
Ditto, with scolloped drawers below, and shell drawers above - -	13	10	0	9	10	0	4	0	0
Ditto, with column drawers and sliding prospect	13	0	0	9	0	0	4	0	0
Ditto, with column drawers - -	12	10	0	8	10	0	3	10	0
Ditto, with two rows of scolloped drawers	11	15	0	8	0	0	3	5	0
Ditto, with a prospect and swelled brackets	11	0	0	7	10	0	3	0	0
Ditto, without a prospect and straight brackets	10	0	0	7	0	0	2	10	0

Add for quarter columns, 10s. -

✻✻✻✻✻✻✻✻✻✻✻✻✻✻✻✻✻✻✻✻✻✻✻✻✻✻✻✻✻✻✻

BOOK-CASES.

	£.	s.	d.	£.	s.	d.	£.	s.	d.
Book-case with dentils, and fret -	7	10	0	5	0	0	2	5	0
Ditto, square head, pannel or sash doors, with sliding shelves only - -	6	0	0	4	0	0	1	15	0

	£.	s.	d.	£.	s.	d.	£.	s.	d.
Book-case, pitch pediment head, without dentils or fret and plain balls - -	7	10	0	5	0	0	2	5	0
Ditto, with dentils, fret and shield -	10	0	0	7	0	0	3	0	0
Ditto, with arch doors - -	10	10	0	7	10	0	3	5	0
Ditto, with scolloped doors -	11	0	0	8	0	0	3	5	0
Ditto, with Chinese doors - -	12	0	0	9	0	0	3	10	0
Ditto, with scroll pediment head and pannel doors - - - -	12	0	0	9	0	0	3	10	0
Ditto, with Chinese doors -	13	0	0	10	0	0	4	0	0
Add for quarter columns, 20 s. -							0	10	0

N. B. The above doors are without glazing; carved work not to exceed 25 s.

HIGH CHEST OF DRAWERS.

	£.	s.	d.	£.	s.	d.	£.	s.	d.
Chest on a frame, square head and corners and plain feet - - -	13	0	0	9	0	0	3	10	0
Table to suit ditto - - -	4	10	0	2	15	0	1	5	0

	£.	ſ.	d.	£.	ſ.	d.	£.	ſ.	d.
Ditto, drawers, cheſt on cheſt, and ſwelled brackets - - - -	13	0	0	9	0	0	3	10	0
Table to ſuit ditto - - -	5	0	0	3	5	0	1	7	6
Ditto, drawers on a frame, claw feet, and quarter columns - - -	15	0	0	11	0	0	4	0	0
A table to ſuit ditto - - -	5	0	0	3	15	0	1	7	6
Ditto, drawers, cheſt on cheſt, and ſwelled brackets - - -	15	0	0	10	10	0	4	0	0
Table to ſuit ditto - - -	6	0	0	4	0	0	1	10	0
Ditto, drawers, pitch pediment head, ſquare corners, plain feet, without dentils or fret, and plain balls - - -	16	0	0	11	10	0	4	0	0
Table to ſuit ditto - - -	4	0	0	2	15	0	1	5	0
Ditto, drawers, cheſt on cheſt -	16	0	0	11	10	0	4	0	0
Table to ſuit ditto, with ſtraight brackets	5	0	0	3	0	0	1	5	0
Ditto, drawers with quarter columns	17	0	0	12	10	0	4	10	0
Table to ſuit ditto - - -	6	0	0	4	0	0	1	10	0

	£.	s.	d.	£.	s.	d.	£.	s.	d.
Ditto drawers, on a frame, and claw feet	17	0	0	13	0	0	4	10	0
Table to suit ditto — —	5	0	0	3	5	0	1	5	0
Ditto, drawers with dentils, fret and shield	19	0	0	14	0	0	5	0	0
Table to suit ditto — —	6	0	0	4	0	0	1	10	0
Ditto, drawers, chest on chest —	20	0	0	15	0	0	5	0	0
Table to suit ditto — —	6	0	0	4	0	0	1	10	0
Chest on a frame, claw feet, leaves on the knees, and shell drawer, in the frame	20	0	0	15	0	0	5	0	0
Table to suit ditto — —	6	0	0	4	0	0	1	10	0
Ditto, drawers, scroll pediment head, carved work not to exceed, £.3 10s.	21	0	0	16	0	0	5	10	0
Table to suit ditto — —	6	0	0	4	0	0	1	10	0
Ditto, drawers, chest on chest —	21	0	0	16	0	0	5	10	0
Table to suit ditto — —	6	0	0	4	0	0	1	10	0
Add for a desk drawer to any of the above drawers £.3 — —									

	£.	s.	d.	£.	s.	d.	£.	s.	d.
Low chest of drawers with three long and five small drawers - -				4	10	0	1	12	6
Ditto, with four long, and five small drawers				5	0	0	1	15	0
Ditto, on frame, 18 inches high, without a drawer - - - -				5	10	0	1	17	6

CHAIRS with CROOKED LEGS.

	£.	s.	d.	£.	s.	d.	£.	s.	d.
Chair with plain feet, and banister with leather bottoms - - -	1	14	0	1	5	0	0	9	0
Arm ditto - - -	2	18	0	2	5	0	0	16	0
Ditto with cut through banister -	1	16	0	1	7	0	0	10	0
Arm ditto - - -	3	0	0	2	12	0	0	17	0
Ditto, with claw feet - -	2	0	0	1	10	0	0	10	0
Arm ditto - - -	3	3	0	2	13	0	0	17	0
Ditto, with shells on the knees, and front rail	2	3	0	1	13	0	0	10	0
Arm ditto - - -	3	7	6	2	16	0	0	17	0

	£.	s.	d.	£.	s.	d.	£.	s.	d.
Ditto, with leaves on the knees - -	2	6	0	1	15	0	0	10	0
Arm ditto - - -	3	11	0	2	18	0	0	17	0
Ditto with fluted or ogee backs -	2	10	0	1	15	0	0	10	0
Arm ditto - - -	3	15	0	3	0	0	0	17	0
For relieving the banisters, add according to the work on them.									
For any extraordinary carved work, add in proportion.									
For damask bottoms add 2 s.									
For hair add 2 s. 6 d.									
Add to an arm chair made for a close stool, with a cover to the pan, framed, 7 s. 6 d.							0	3	9
Ditto, not framed, 5 s.							0	2	6

CHAIRS MARLBOROUGH FEET.

	£.	s.	d.	£.	s.	d.	£.	s.	d.
chair, plain open banister, without bases or brackets, with leather bottoms -	1	12	0	1	5	0	0	9	0

	£.	s.	d.	£.	s.	d.	£.	s.	d.
Arm ditto - - -	2	18	0	2	5	0	0	16	0
Ditto, with fluted or ogee backs, bases and brackets - - -	2	5	0	1	15	0	0	10	0
Arm ditto - - -	3	10	0	2	15	0	0	17	0

Add, for relieving the banister, and for damask or hair bottoms, or a close-stool, as in the crooked leg chairs.

For any chair as above, stuffed over the rail, and brass nails, add 8 s.

For fluted or ogee back feet, add to the journeyman, 1 s.

CORNER CHAIR for CLOSE-STOOL.

	£.	s.	d.	£.	s.	d.	£.	s.	d.
Corner chair, plain feet, and banister	2	10	0	2	0	0	0	12	6
Ditto, claw feet and open banisters -	3	10	0	2	15	0	0	14	0

	£	s.	d.	£	s.	d.	£	s.	d.
Corner chair, with the upper part of the legs worked crooked	3	15	0	3	0	0	0	16	6
For commode front, add	0	12	0	0	10	0	0	5	0

✿✿✿✿✿✿✿✿✿✿✿✿✿✿✿✿✿✿✿✿✿✿✿✿✿✿✿✿

EASY CHAIR.

	£	s.	d.	£	s.	d.	£	s.	d.
Easy chair frame, plain feet and knees, without casters	2	10	0	2	5	0	0	18	0
Ditto with claw feet	2	15	0	2	10	0	0	18	0
Ditto, with claw feet and leaves on knees	3	5	0	3	0	0	0	18	0
Ditto, Marlborough feet, bases and brackets	2	10	0	2	5	0	0	18	0
CHAIR FRAME for stuffing over back and seat, with Marlborough feet	1	5	0	1	0	0	0	6	0
Arm ditto	2	0	0	1	10	0	0	10	0
Folding cabbin chair frame, for stuffing	1	5	0	1	0	0	0	6	0
Ditto, stools	0	12	0	0	8	0	0	2	0
Ditto, of oak				0	5	0	0	1	6

B

	£.	s.	d.	£.	s.	d.	£.	s.	d.
Add for brackets to any chair — —	0	2	6	0	2	6	0	1	3
And bases to any chair, is — —	0	2	6	0	2	6	0	1	3
Add for carved mouldings —	0	12	0	0	12	0	0	1	3

✻✻✻✻✻✻✻✻✻✻✻✻✻✻✻✻✻✻✻✻✻✻✻✻✻✻✻✻✻✻

SOFFAS MARLBOROUGH FEET.

	£.	s.	d.	£.	s.	d.	£.	s.	d.
Soffa, plain feet and rails without casters	4	10	0	4	0	0	1	0	0
Ditto, with bases and brackets —	5	0	0	4	10	0	1	5	0
Ditto, with a fret on the feet — —	7	10	0	7	0	0	1	15	0
Ditto, with a fret on feet and rails, and carved mouldings — —	10	10	0	9	10	0	2	10	0

✕✕✕✕✕✕✕✕✕✕✕✕✕✕✕✕✕✕✕✕✕✕✕✕✕✕

SOFFAS with CROOKED LEGS.

	£.	s.	d.	£.	s.	d.	£.	s.	d.
Soffa, plain feet and knees, without casters,	5	0	0	4	10	0	1	5	0

	£	s.	d.	£	s.	d.	£	s.	d.
Soffa, claw feet - - -	5	10	0	5	0	0	1	5	0
Ditto, with leaves on the knees -	6	10	0	6	0	0	1	5	0
Ditto, with carved mouldings -	7	10	0	7	0	0	1	7	6
Add for casters, 10s.									

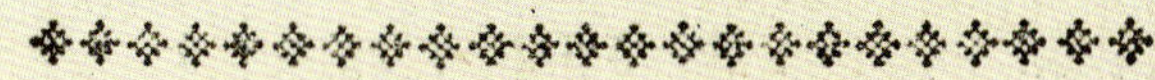

S E T T E E S.

	£	s.	d.	£	s.	d.	£	s.	d.
Settees, plain crooked legs feet and banisters, without casters, with hair or damask bottom	6	10	0	5	0	0	1	6	0
Ditto, Marlborough, with bases and brackets cut through banisters - -	6	10	0	5	0	0	1	6	0
Ditto, with claw feet and knees carved	8	0	0	5	15	0	1	6	0
Ditto, with fluted or ogee backs -	8	10	0	6	5	0	1	8	0
Add for carved moulding 20s. and to the journeyman - - -							0	2	0

COUCHES with CROOKED LEGS.

	£	s.	d.	£	s.	d.	£	s.	d.
Couch frame, plain knees, feet, and banisters, without bottom or casters -	4	10	0	3	0	0	1	4	0
Ditto, with claw feet and open banister	5	5	0	3	15	0	1	4	0
Ditto, with leaves on the knees - -	6	0	0	4	10	0	1	4	0
Ditto with fluted or ogee backs -	6	5	0	4	15	0	1	5	0
Ditto, with Marlborough feet, without bases or brackets - -	4	10	0	3	0	0	1	0	0
Ditto, with bases and brackets -	5	0	0	3	10	0	1	4	0
Ditto, with fluted or ogee backs -	5	5	0	3	15	0	1	6	0
Add for carved moulding, 20s. and to the journeyman - - -							0	2	0

DINING TABLES.

	£	s.	d.	£	s.	d.	£	s.	d.
Dining Table, plain feet, crooked, or Marlborough, with bases, 3 feet in the bed	3	5	0	1	17	6	0	17	6

	£.	s.	d.	£.	s.	d	£.	s.	d.
Ditto, 3 feet 6 inches - -	4	0	0	2	5	0	1	0	0
Ditto, 4 feet - - -	4	10	0	2	15	0	1	2	6
Ditto, 4 feet 6 inches - -	5	0	0	3	10	0	1	5	0
Ditto, 5 feet with 6 legs - -	6	10	0	4	10	0	1	15	0
Ditto, 5 feet 6 inches, with 8 legs -	8	6	0	5	15	0	2	5	0

For tables with claw feet, add 2 s. 6 d. *per* claw.

For tables with straight legs, without bales, deduct 5 s. and 3 s. in journeyman's wages.

❖∞∞∞∞∞∞∞∞∞∞∞∞∞∞∞∞∞∞∞∞∞∞∞∞∞∞∞❖

CARD TABLES with CROOKED LEGS.

	£.	s.	d.	£.	s.	d	£.	s.	d.
Card table, plain feet and knees -	3	10	0	2	5	0	0	17	6
Ditto, with claw feet, - -	4	0	0	2	15	0	0	17	6
Ditto, with carved knees and mouldings	5	0	0	3	15	0	0	18	6

Add for covering, without finding the cloth, 7 s. 6 d. and to the journeyman for sinking the top, 2 s. 6 d.

	£. s. d.	£. s. d.	£. s. d.
Card table, with a drawer, without bases or brackets - - -	3 0 0	2 0 0	0 15 0
Ditto, with bases and brackets -	3 10 0	2 5 0	0 17 6
Ditto, with a carved moulding, - -	4 0 0	2 15 0	0 17 6
Add for clamping the tops, 10s. and to the jouneyman, 5s.			

❖❖❖❖❖❖❖❖❖

CARD TABLES with ROUND CORNERS.

	£. s. d.		£. s. d.
Claw feet and plain knees - -	5 0 0		1 2 6
Ditto, lined with green cloth -	6 10 0		1 10 0
Ditto, leaves on knees and carved mouldings	8 0 0		1 10 0
Ditto, with carved rails - -	10 0 0		2 0 0

PEMBROKE or BREAKFAST TABLES.

	£. s. d.	£. s. d.	£. s. d.
Breakfast table plain - -	2 15 0	1 15 0	0 12 6
Ditto, with a drawer - - -	3 0 0	2 0 0	0 14 6

	£.	s.	d.	£.	s.	d.	£.	s.	d.
Breakfast table, with bases and brackets	3	5	0	2	5	0	0	17	6
Ditto, with a plain stretcher — —	3	10	0	2	10	0	1	0	0
Ditto, with open stretcher and two drawers	4	0	0	3	0	0	1	2	6
Ditto, with crooked legs and plain feet	3	5	0	2	5	0	0	17	6
Ditto, with claw feet — —	3	15	0	2	15	0	0	17	6
Add for scolloping the top, 4s. and to the journeyman — — — —							0	2	0

CORNER TABLES.

	£.	s.	d.	£.	s.	d.	£.	s.	d.
Corner table, crooked legs, or Marlborough feet, with bases three feet square	3	10	0	2	10	0	1	0	0
Ditto, claw feet — — —	4	10	0	3	0	0	1	0	0

TEA TABLES.

	£.	s.	d.	£.	s.	d.	£.	s.	d.
Plain top and feet — —	2	15	0	1	15	0	0	12	6

	£.	s.	d.	£.	s.	d.	£.	s.	d.
Plain tea table with claw feet - -	3	5	0	2	5	0	0	12	6
Ditto, leaves on the knees - -	4	0	0	2	15	0	0	12	6
Ditto, ſcolloped top and carved pillar	5	15	0				1	2	6
Add for fluting the pillar, 5s. for journeyman							0	2	6

FOLDING STANDS.

	£.	s.	d.	£.	s.	d.	£.	s.	d.
Stand 22 inches diameter, with a box, plain top and feet - - -	1	15	0	1	5	0	0	11	0
Ditto, plain top and claw feet -	2	2	6	1	12	6	0	11	0
Ditto, with leaves on the knees - -	2	10	0	2	0	0	0	11	0
Ditto, fixed 18 inches - -	1	4	0	0	16	0	0	7	6
Add for fluting the pillar, 5s. and to the journeyman - - -							0	2	6

SIDE-BOARD TABLES.

	£.	s.	d.	£.	s.	d.	£.	s.	d.
Side-board tables, with baſes and brackets, ſix feet by two feet ſix inches - -	5	0	0	3	0	0	1	2	0

	£.	s.	d.	£.	s.	d.	£.	s.	d.
Five feet by 2 feet 6 inches - -	4	5	0	2	10	0	0	18	6
Four feet 6 inches by 2 feet 6 inches -	3	10	0	2	5	0	0	16	0
Four feet by 2 feet 6 inches -	3	5	0	2	0	0	0	14	0
Three feet 6 inches by 2 feet 3 inches	3	0	0	1	15	0	0	12	0
Add for carved mouldings 2s. *per* foot, for fret round the rails 5s. *per* foot, and to the journeyman - - -							0	2	6

✳✳✳✳✳✳✳✳✳✳✳✳✳✳✳✳✳✳✳✳✳✳✳✳✳✳✳✳✳

TEA KETTLE STANDS.

	£.	s.	d.	£.	s.	d.	£.	s.	d.
Tea kettle stand, with gallery top and plain feet	2	10	0				0	15	0
Ditto with claw feet, leaves on knees, carved and fluted pillar, with turned banisters	3	10	0				0	15	0
Bason Stand, with three pillars & two drawers	2	10	0	1	15	0	0	15	0
Ditto, square, with two drawers -	1	10	0	1	2	6	0	12	0

C

SQUARE TEA TABLES.

	£.	s.	d.	£.	s.	d.	£.	s.	d.
Tea table, square top, plain feet and rails	3	0	0	2	5	0	1	5	0
Ditto, claw feet - - -	3	10	0	2	15	0	1	5	0
Ditto, leaves on the knees -	4	10	0	3	10	0	1	5	0
Ditto, with carved rails - -	6	0	0				1	5	0

XXXXXXXXXXXXXXXXXXXXXXXXXXXXXXXXX

COMMODE DRESSING TABLE.

	£.	s.	d.	£.	s.	d.	£.	s.	d.
Commode dressing table, with four long drawers, without a dressing drawer -	14	0	0				4	10	0

Add for a dressing drawer from 30 to 80 shillings, and for journeyman's wages in proportion.

WRITING TABLES.

	£ s. d.	£ s. d.	£ s. d.
Writing table, with one top to raise on one side only front to draw out - -	7 0 0	5 0 0	1 12 6
Ditto, with one top to raise on both sides	7 10 0	5 10 0	2 0 0
Ditto, with two tops to raise on both sides	8 0 0	6 0 0	2 0 0
Work in the drawer excluded.			

BUREAU TABLES.

	£ s. d.	£ s. d.	£ s. d.
Bureau table, with prospect door, and square corners - - -	7 10 0	6 0 0	2 7 6
Ditto, with quarter columns - -	8 10 0	7 0 0	2 15 0

CHINA TABLES.

	£ s. d.	£ s. d.	£ s. d.
China table, plain legs and stretcher, three feet long with bases, brackets, and a fret top	4 10 0		1 15 0

	£.	s.	d.	£.	s.	d.	£.	s.	d.
China table, open stretcher, top three feet long bases and brackets - -	5	0	0				1	15	0
Ditto, with fret frame - -	8	0	0				3	10	0
Add for commode ditto £.2 10s. To journeyman, - -							1	15	0

❖❖❖❖❖❖❖❖❖❖❖❖❖❖❖❖❖❖❖❖❖❖❖❖❖❖❖❖❖❖❖❖❖❖❖❖

PLAIN NIGHT TABLE.

	£.	s.	d.	£.	s.	d.	£.	s.	d.
Plain night table - - -	4	0	0	3	5	0	1	5	0

FRAMES for MARBLE SLABS.

	£.	s.	d.	£.	s.	d.	£.	s.	d.
Frame for marble slab, Marlborough feet, without bases or brackets, about 4 feet long	2	10	0	1	10	0	0	12	0
Ditto, with bases and brackets, commode rails	3	10	0				0	17	0
Ditto, with plain knees and claw feet	4	0	0				1	0	0
Ditto, with leaves on the knees and carved mouldings - - -	5	0	0				1	0	0

PINE KITCHEN TABLES.

	£.	s.	d.	£.	s.	d.	£.	s.	d.
Pine kitchen table, full frame, with two leaves hung with rule joint, 4 feet long, and two drawers - - -				1	17	6	0	15	0
Ditto, with one leaf and one drawer				1	10	0	0	12	6
Ditto, 3 feet 6 inches long, with two leaves				1	10	0	0	12	6
Ditto, with one leaf - -				1	5	0	0	10	0
Ditto, single frame, three feet six inches, with drawer - - -				0	16	0	0	7	0
Ditto, without a drawer - -				0	12	0	0	5	0

XXXXXXXXXXXXXXXXXXXXXXXXXXXXXXXXXXXXXXXXX

JOINT STOOL.

	£.	s.	d.	£.	s.	d.	£.	s.	d.
Joint stool with a drawer and sliding top three feet long - - -				0	12	0	0	5	6
Ditto, without a drawer -				0	10	0	0	4	6
Ditto, fixed, with a drawer - -				0	10	0	0	4	6

	£.	s.	d.	£.	s.	d.	£.	s.	d.
Joint stool fixed without a drawer -				0	7	6	0	3	3
Stool for a store of walnut - -				0	12	0	0	5	6
Ditto, of pine - -				0	7	0	0	3	0

FIRE SCREENS.

	£.	s.	d.	£.	s.	d.	£.	s.	d.
Fire screen, with plain feet - -	1	15	0	1	5	0	0	11	0
Ditto, with claw feet - -	2	2	6	1	12	6	0	11	0
Ditto, with leaves on the knees -	2	10	0	2	0	0	0	11	0
Add for fluting the pillar 5s. and to the jour-									
neyman - - -							0	2	6
HORSE FIRE Screens without a fret	2	10	0	2	5	0	0	17	6
Ditto, with a fret under the stretcher	3	0	0	2	15	0	1	5	0

DUMB WAITERS.

	£.	s.	d.	£.	s.	d.	£.	s.	d.
Dumb waiter with four tops plain feet	5	0	0				1	0	0

	£.	s.	d.	£.	s.	d.	£.	s.	d.
Dumb Waiter with claw feet - -	5	10	0				1	0	0
Ditto, with leaves on the knees -	6	0	0				1	0	0

CLOATHS PRESSES.

	£.	s.	d.	£.	s.	d.	£.	s.	d.
Cloaths press in two parts, upper part about 4 feet square in the front, the doors hung with rule joints and sliding shelves, with 3 drawers in the lower part, inside work of red cedar	15	0	0	11	0	0	3	10	0
Ditto inside work, not red cedar -	13	10	0	9	10	0	3	10	0
Ditto, in one part without drawers, inside work of red cedar - - -	12	0	0	8	0	0	2	10	0
Ditto, inside work not red cedar -	10	10	0	7	10	0	2	10	0
Ditto, with two drawers inside below, and pins above, with doors hung in the common way	8	10	0	6	0	0	2	0	0
Ditto, of pine - - -				4	0	0	1	10	0

	£.	s.	d.	£.	s.	d.	£.	s.	d.
Add to any of the above presses with a pitch pediment, dentils, fret and shield —	6	0	0	5	0	0	2	0	0
Ditto, without dentils, fret or shield —	0	10	0	2	10	0	1	2	6

❋❋❋❋❋❋❋❋❋❋❋❋❋❋❋❋❋❋❋❋❋❋❋❋❋❋❋❋

CORNER CUPBOARDS.

	£.	s.	d.	£.	s.	d.	£.	s.	d.
Corner cupboard, in two parts, about 7 feet high, square head, and straight pannels	9	10	0	6	10	0	2	0	0
Ditto with common sash doors — —	9	10	0	6	10	0	2	0	0
Ditto, with square head, dentils and fret, plain pannel doors — — —	10	10	0	7	10	0	2	10	0
Ditto, with common sash doors —	10	10	0	7	10	0	2	10	0
Ditto, with scroll pediment head, dentil cornice, fret, shield, roses and blazes, with plain pannel doors — — —	15	0	0	10	10	6	3	0	0
Ditto, with common sash doors —	14	0	0	10	10	0	3	0	0

	£ s. d.	£ s. d.	£ s. d.
Corner cupboard with scolloped doors, and flat pannels - - -	16 0 0	11 10 0	3 10 0
Ditto, with Chinese doors - -	15 10 0	11 10 0	4 0 0
Deduct in a pitch pediment for any of the above cupboards, 15s. and to the journeyman			0 7 6

❊❊❊❊❊❊❊❊❊❊❊❊❊❊❊❊❊❊❊❊❊❊❊❊❊❊❊❊❊

SINGLE CUPBOARDS.

	£ s. d.	£ s. d.	£ s. d.
Cupboard, about four feet high, and three feet wide, square head, and common sash doors	4 15 0	3 15 0	1 5 0
Ditto, with plain pannels - -	4 15 0	3 15 0	1 5 0
Ditto, with dentil cornice, plain pannels	5 10 0	4 0 0	1 10 0
Ditto, with common sash doors -	5 10 0	4 0 0	1 10 0

PINE CUPBOARDS.

	£ s. d.	£ s. d.
Double pine cupboard, about 7 feet high	4 10 0	1 5 0

	£. s. d.	£. s. d.	£. s. d.
Single pine cupboard, about four feet high and three feet wide - -		2 0 0	0 15 0
The prices to any of the cupboards, are without painting or glazing - -			

CLOCK CASES.

	£. s. d.	£. s. d.	£. s. d.
Clock cases with square head and corners	6 0 0	4 0 0	1 15 0
Ditto, with scroll pediment head, without fret, dentils or carved work, and square corners	8 0 0	5 0 0	2 5 0
Ditto, with column corners - -	10 0 0	7 0 0	3 0 0
Ditto, with fret, dentils, shield, roses and blazes	12 0 0	9 0 0	4 0 0
Ditto, without fret or dentils -	11 0 0	8 0 0	3 5 0

The above prices without glazing.

	£. s. d.	£. s. d.	£. s. d.
CRADLE PLAIN without carving -	2 15 0	1 10 0	0 12 6

	£	s.	d.	£	s.	d.	£	s.	d.
Bedstead with low posts, two feet posts, mahogony claw feet, and plain knees	2	5	0				0	10	0
Ditto, high posts, all poplar, stained except feet posts of mahogony, claw feet and plain knees	4	0	0				0	12	0
Ditto, all mahogony, claw feet and plain knees	7	0	0				1	0	0
Ditto, head posts poplar - -	6	10	0				0	15	0
Ditto, claw feet, leaves on the knees, not fluted with brass caps - -	8	0	0				1	0	0
Ditto, knees to move, fluted pillars, a member carved on capital and base - -	10	0	0				1	10	0
GOTHIC PILLARS and strait feet bedsteads									
Bedstead poplar stained two feet posts									
Mahogony with bases - -	3	0	0				0	12	0
Ditto, all mahogony plain turned pillars & bases	5	10	0				0	15	0
Ditto,, Gothic pillars and fretton feet	10	10	0				2	10	0
Mahogony Field Bedsteads with canopy rails - - -	6	0	0				1	0	0

	£	s.	d.	£	s.	d.	£	s.	d.
Poplar corded bedstead - -				0	18	0	0	5	0
Cott ditto - - -				0	18	0	0	5	0
Ditto, low posts with four screws -				1	5	0	0	7	0
Ditto, claw feet to two posts - -				2	0	0	0	9	0
Ditto, high posts, plain turned -				1	17	6	0	9	0
Ditto, with bases and caps, claw feet				2	12	6	0	12	6
POPLAR FIELD BEDSTEAD, canopy rails				2	15	0	0	13	0
Ditto, strait rails - -				2	0	0	0	10	0
Add for fluting the feet posts, 15s. and to the journeyman 7s. 6d. - -									
Add for casters to any of the above									

✻✻✻✻✻✻✻✻✻✻✻✻✻✻✻✻✻✻✻✻✻✻✻✻✻✻

CHINA TRAYS.

	£	s.	d.	£	s.	d.	£	s.	d.
Fret China tray, 18 inches by 24 -	1	15	0				0	18	0
Commode ditto - - -	2	15	0				1	8	0

	£.	s.	d.	£.	s.	d.	£.	s.	d.
Tray for pewter, 18 inches by 24 -	1	0	0	0	14	0	0	4	6
Ditto, for knives and forks 15 inches by 9	0	10	0	0	7	0	0	3	0

XXXXXXXXXXXXXXXXXXXXXXXXXXXXXXXXXXXXXXXXXXXXXX

TEA BOARDS.

	£.	s.	d.	£.	s.	d.	£.	s.	d.
TEA BOARDS scolloped at 15*d. per* inch							0	7	6
Ditto, plain turned, from 15 to 22 inches, at 6*d per* inch - - -									
Hand boards, from 6 to 12 inches, at 4*d. per* inch - - -									
Decanter stands lined, at 5*s per* pair -									

CORNICES.

	£.	s.	d.	£.	s.	d.	£.	s.	d.
Bed cornice of cedar, cut open for carving or covering, with the pullies to the rails				1	10	0	0	10	0

	£.	s.	d.	£.	s.	d.	£.	s.	d.
Window cornice, with pullies				0	10	0	0	3	4
Bed ditto, scolloped on the upper edge				1	0	0	0	6	0
Window ditto				0	6	0	0	1	6
Bed ditto, plain, with pieces to the corners				1	0	0	0	6	0
Window ditto				0	6	0	0	2	0
Bed ditto, flat scolloped on the upper edge				0	15	0	0	4	6
Window ditto				0	5	0	0	1	3

Add for pullies to the rails, of the above bed cornices, 5s. and to the window, ditto, 2s.

W I N D O W   B L I N D S.

	£.	s.	d.	£.	s.	d.	£.	s.	d.
Window blinds for four light windows	0	11	0	0	6	6	0	2	6
Ditto, for three light windows	0	9	0	0	5	0	0	2	0

Add for canvas, *per* yard 3s. 6d.

	£. s. d.	£. s. d.	£. s. d.
Plain bed rails with pullies - -		0 10 0	
Window ditto without hooks -		0 3 6	
Bed ditto without pullies - -		0 5 0	

STORE DOUBLE DESK.

	£. s. d.	£. s. d.	£. s. d.
Store double desk of walnut, four feet square on a frame, with one row of drawers, and pigeon holes - - -		6 10 0	2 5 0
Ditto, of pine - - -		4 10 0	1 10 6
Ditto, single, three feet 6 inches, long with drawers and pigeon holes - -		2 10 0	0 18 0
Ditto, with two drawers only, without pigeon holes - - - -		2 0 0	0 15 0

	£. s. d.	£. s. d.	£. s. d.
Screens, to stand round the fire, framed with half inch pannels, 6 feet 2 inches high, 2 feet 2 inches wide, 10s. *per* leaf -			

❖—┼—oooo—┼—oooo—┼—oooo—┼—oooo—┼—oooo—┼—oooo—┼—oooo—┼—oooo—┼—oooo—┼—❖

PICTURE FRAMES.

	£. s. d.	£. s. d.	£. s. d.
Picture frames stained black, 4 feet by 3 feet 4 inches, without carved work - -		1 15 0	0 12 6
Ditto, 2 feet 6 inches, by 2 feet 1 inch		1 5 0	0 7 6
Ditto, for pasting, 6 feet by 2 feet 2 inches, with board backs, or straining frames without canvas - - -		0 15 0	0 7 6
Ditto, 4 feet by 1 foot 8 inches -		0 8 0	0 3 9
Ditto, for glass, 14 inches by 11 inches		0 4 0	0 1 6
Ditto, 12 inches by 10 - -		0 3 6	0 1 3
Ditto, for pasting on the back of the frame, 2 feet by 18 inches - - -		0 2 0	0 0 9

	£ s. d.	£ s. d.	£ s. d.
Ditto, with a back board — -		0 5 0	0 2 3
Ditto, 15 inches by 10 inches -		0 1 6	0 0 0
Ditto, for maps framed top and bottom only		0 3 9	

XXXXXXXXXXXXXXXXXXXXXXXXXXXXXXXXX

IRONING BOARDS.

	£ s. d.	£ s. d.	£ s. d.
Ironing boards of cedar, 6 feet by 4 feet		0 15 0	0 3 9
Ditto, 5 feet by 3 feet 6 inches -		0 10 0	0 3 0
Ditto, 4 feet by 3 feet - -		0 7 6	0 2 6
Add for truffels 5s. -			

CHESTS.

	£ s. d.	£ s. d.	£ s. d.
Chest, 3 feet 6 inches by 1 foot 6 inches in the top, hung with snip bills and common lock		1 6 0	0 6 0

CHESTS.

	£.	s.	d.	£.	s.	d.	£.	s.	d.
Chests, 4 feet long by 21 inches wide in top, with 2 drawers and brackets -				2	0	0	0	12	6
Ditto, without drawers or brackets,				1	7	6	0	6	6
Ditto, of walnut - - - -				2	0	0	0	12	6
Ditto, with brackets and drawers, -				3	0	0	0	17	6
Ditto, of red cedar, without drawers or brackets	3	0	0				0	12	6
Ditto, with drawers and brackets -	5	0	0				0	17	6
Mahogony the same as red cedar -									

❖❖❖❖❖❖❖❖❖❖❖❖❖❖❖❖❖❖❖❖❖❖❖❖❖❖❖❖❖❖

BOTTLE CASES.

	£.	s.	d.	£.	s.	d.	£.	s.	d.
Bottle case of Mahogony or walnut for 12 bottles, with brackets, - - -	3	0	0	2	0	0	0	15	0
Ditto, of pine - - -				0	16	0	0	5	0

	£	s.	d.	£	s.	d.	£	s.	d.
Chair claws, or table ditto, at 1s. 6d. each									
Ditto, for tea tables, at 2s. each									
Ditto, for drawers, at 2s. each									
Ditto, for bedsteads, at 2s. 6d. each									
Ditto, for stands, at 1s. 9d. each									

✳✳✳✳✳✳✳✳✳✳✳✳✳✳✳✳✳✳✳✳✳✳✳✳✳✳✳✳✳

COFFINS.

	£	s.	d.	£	s.	d.	£	s.	d.
Coffin for a grown person, flat top, tin handles				2	10	0			
Ditto, ridged top				3	0	0			
Ditto, with lacquered or silver handles	7	0	0	3	10	0			
Ditto, with letters	7	10	0	4	0	0			
Ditto, with letters, and lace round the bottom only	8	0	0	4	10	0			
Ditto, with three plates without lace	8	10	0	5	0	0			
Ditto, with lace round the bottom only	9	0	0	5	10	0			

	£	s.	d.	£	s.	d.	£	s.	d.
Coffin full trimmed	10	0	0						
Ditto, covered with black cloth, lined with flannel, made of pine	15	0	0						
Ditto, of red cedar	17	0	0						
Pine ditto, flat top, stained tin handles				1	5	0			
Ditto, ridged top				1	15	0			
Ditto, without colouring or handles				0	15	0			

Children's coffins in proportion to grown persons, at six feet.

Note, *Red cedar the same as mahogony.*

Deduct for a covered coffin, without lace, for a grown person, 40 s. and with lace, round the bottom only, 30 s. and in proportion for children's.